D1711688

Sports Stars

MIKE SCHMIDT

The Human Vacuum Cleaner

By Mike Herbert

 CHILDRENS PRESS, CHICAGO

Cover photograph: Howard Zryb
Inside photographs courtesy of the following:
Howard Zryb, page 10
© 1982—O.C. Shaw, Creative Intrusions, pages 15, 26, 40, and 43
Ira Golden, pages 12, 35, and 38
Steve Schwartz, pages 17 and 32
Kevin W. Reece, page 21

Library of Congress Cataloging in Publication Data

Herbert, Mike.
  Mike Schmidt, the human vacuum cleaner.

  (Sport stars)
  Summary: A brief biography of the star baseball player for
the Philadelphia Phillies.
  1. Schmidt, Mike, 1949-   —Juvenile literature.
2. Baseball players—United States—Biography—Juvenile
literature. [1. Schmidt, Mike, 1949-   . 2. Baseball players]
I. Title. II. Series.
GV865.S36H37 1983   796.357'092'4 [B] [92] 83-7621
ISBN 0-516-04332-3

    2 3 4 5 6 7 8 9 10 11 12 R 90 89 88 87 86 85 84

Sports Stars

MIKE SCHMIDT

The Human Vacuum Cleaner

One of the things Mike does well is hit home runs.

Mike Schmidt hits home runs. He is a star baseball player. He hits smashing home runs that make the outfield seats rattle. He hits long, high home runs. Fans in the stands try to catch them. Mike Schmidt loves to hit home runs. In the last eight years no one has hit more home runs than he has.

Some home run hitters aren't good all-around baseball players. Some home run hitters strike out too much. Mike used to be like that. Now he is a complete baseball player. Many experts say he is the best all-around player in baseball.

Mike is 6 feet 2 inches tall and weighs about 200 pounds.

Catcher Tim McCarver, a former player with the St. Louis Cardinals and the Philadelphia Phillies, says, "He is the best player in the game today."

Mike Schmidt grew up in Dayton, Ohio. His family was not rich and it was not poor. But Mike admits he was spoiled as a kid. He says he had everything he needed from a small family and loving parents.

Mike's friends played sports. So did Mike.

"I had a lot of nice friends," said Mike. "We had a very nice park to play ball in. We played football. We played basketball. We played baseball, of course. We played golf with a 7-iron from tree to tree. We played sunup to sundown."

When he was about eight years old, a very scary thing happened to him. He was hit by lightning. But Mike was not injured badly. He was very lucky.

When Mike was a very young boy he loved baseball. And people helped him play the game. His grandmother used to throw Whiffle Balls to him. He could hit them pretty well when he was only four or five years old. Mike played Little League baseball too.

Mike's grandmother died of cancer on Mike's 31st birthday. She was his Number 1 fan. She encouraged him to play baseball. She pushed him to concentrate on the game. She died before he won his first Most Valuable Player Award.

Mike is disappointed she didn't see her grandson win one of baseball's major awards.

"My mom and dad have always been behind me 100 percent," says Mike. "My dad used to give me five dollars a day to go to an electric batting machine. I used to hit $2.50 left-handed and $2.50 right-handed. Then I'd go to work at a swimming pool."

Mike was a switch hitter then. He batted both right-handed and left-handed. In college he decided to hit only right-handed. "That was probably the turning point of my career," Mike says.

"I went to Fairview High School," said Mike.

"The sports programs were very good. I had good coaching. I played football, basketball, and baseball in the Dayton Public League. It was a very strong sports league, with a lot of good competition."

Mike had fun in sports. But he was not always lucky. He was a quarterback in football. He hurt his knee in his second year of high school. The doctor had to operate so Mike could keep playing. He decided to play some more.

Then, in his last year of high school, he hurt his *other* knee playing football. Again the doctor told Mike he had to operate so Mike could keep playing sports. And again Mike had to exercise his knee to make it strong.

Mike and Willie Montenez, a former Phillies player,
know their team is doing well.

"My knees really held me back as a young ballplayer," said Mike.

But Mike was named an honorable mention, All-City baseball player in high school. He played against Steve Yeager, now a catcher with the Los Angeles Dodgers.

"I never seemed to be healthy enough as a young player. I guess it was the Lord's will that I became a healthy player."

Mike had a strong desire to be a professional athlete. "I knew I was going to be a professional athlete," he said. "Nobody is born with more ability to play sports than I had. At a young age I was able to play. Sports, no matter what the season, was the only thing that mattered to me—the only thing."

Mike always had a job when he was a youngster. He was a lifeguard. He was a soda jerk; he scooped ice cream. Mike's father owned a restaurant. Mike worked for his father. He made hamburgers. He cleaned tables. He stocked shelves and made sure there was ice. His father wanted Mike to work and taught Mike to be responsible. After Mike got his driver's license, his father told him that every time Mike asked to get off work he would lose his license for a month. Mike worked and played sports.

Mike decided to go to college. He went to Ohio University in Athens, Ohio. He was a serious student. He wanted to build buildings, so he studied to be an architect. Many nights he stayed up late building models of buildings and finishing projects for his art classes. He is still interested in architecture.

In college, Mike still wanted to play sports. The coaches did not know Mike was a good athlete. He decided not to play football. He decided to try basketball. The basketball coaches did not know him. He wanted to try anyway.

"I was a walk-on for the basketball team," Mike said. That meant he did not have a scholarship. He wanted to try anyway.

"I made the freshman team," said Mike. "Then, at the last minute, I decided that basketball would be too much wear and tear on my knees."

Mike did not play basketball any more. He thought baseball was the best sport for him. The baseball coaches did not give him a scholarship either, but he decided to try out for the team.

There were two baseball teams at Ohio University. One was the varsity. It was for the oldest and best players. The other was the freshman team. It was for boys just starting to play college baseball. "I walked on the baseball field and played shortstop on the freshman team," said Mike.

Mike was not the best shortstop at Ohio University. Rich McKinney was. But McKinney left college to play professional baseball. That made Mike Schmidt the best shortstop at Ohio University. He moved up to the varsity team. He got to play often. He played against the best college baseball teams. That made him a better player.

"I was playing with good athletes," said Mike. "My coaching in college was helpful to my career. It turned me into a prospect, into a great, young player, the type of player the Philadelphia Phillies wanted."

Mike had a good college career. Twice he was named All-America at Ohio University. He played in the College World Series in 1970. That was good because scouts, men who look at young players to find pro baseball stars, saw him play well there.

Soon Mike graduated. His degree was in business administration. But his business was going to be baseball.

He was drafted on the second round of the college draft. His team was the Philadelphia Phillies. But they did not want him to play in Philadelphia. They sent him to their team in

Reading, Pennsylvania, a Class AA Eastern League team. Mike played in 74 games and hit .211. Mike already had big muscles. He was supposed to be a better hitter. The Phillies sent him to their AAA team in Eugene, Oregon. He played 131 games for that team and hit .291. That was much better.

So, at the end of the major league season, the Phillies decided to give Mike a chance to play big-league baseball. He came to the Phillies and played in 13 games. He hit only .206, but he had one home run.

The Phillies had moved Mike. He now played third base. They still thought he was going to be

Playing baseball is something Mike loves to do.

a good player. Mike proved them right. He never played minor league baseball again.

Mike had finally become a big league baseball player. He was now Number 20, the Philadelphia third baseman. His boyhood dreams were real. The Phillies were not a winning team, but they had good, young players. Some other players were Bob Boone, Greg Luzinski, and Larry Bowa. With the help of a lot of other good players, they made the Philadelphia Phillies a winner. "We built the tradition that's in Philadelphia now," says Mike.

But it was not easy. When Mike first came to Philadelphia, he tried to be a great hitter. But he struck out a lot. He swung the bat too hard. In 1973, his rookie year, he had the worst average among big-league regulars—.196. He struck out 136 times. The Phillie fans booed Mike and he felt bad.

The next year, however Mike hit .282. He proved he was a star. Those same fans cheered Mike. Now he is a classic, power hitter with a smooth swing. He entertains Philadelphia fans with his tremendous power and with great fielding plays. The fans say he comes through when it counts. That makes Mike proud.

Mike has been playing for 10 years. He has hit 349 home runs. That is the most for anyone who has ever played for Philadelphia. One windy day in Chicago he hit four home runs in a row in one game against the Cubs. He hits a lot of home runs and very long ones, too.

"Mike wants to hit it all the way out of the stadium," says Larry Bowa, who now plays for the Cubs.

Mike hits a home run once every 15 times he goes to bat. That is very good.

Mike is also a great fielder. He is the best fielding third baseman in the league. Seven times he has won the Gold Glove, the league fielding award. When Mike plays third base, not many hits get past him. He scoops up hits like a vacuum cleaner.

Mike has a great throwing arm. He runs well and is a thinking baseball player.

In 1980 he was voted the best player in the National League. In 1981, he did it again! Only Ernie Banks of the Chicago Cubs, in 1958 and 1959, and Joe Morgan of the Cincinnati Reds, in 1975 and 1976, have done that.

Because he is a complete player, Mike has played in seven All-Star Games. For the last four years he has always been the National League starting third baseman. In the 1980 World Series, when Philadelphia won the World Championship over the Kansas City Royals, Mike Schmidt was the most valuable player.

Why is Mike so good? He is big, 6-foot-2, 203 pounds. And he is strong. He once won the weightlifting competition in the *Superstars*. He is a very talented athlete. He is a fine golfer and tennis player and an expert swimmer.

Mike wants to keep Philadelphia a winner. "I work awfully hard on my physical conditioning," he says. "I study the game of baseball. I love the game. I take a lot of pride in my performance. I love to win. I like to be on a winning team. I'd like to be a baseball manager some day."

Mike's teammate, Pete Rose, says, "Mike's one of the premier players in the game today

because he understands there's more to offense than just swinging for the fences."

That's also what Mike says in his book, *Always on the Offense*. Mike says the question he asks himself when he plays is, "What can I do in this situation that will help my team score runs? It could be a home run, or a bunt, a sacrifice fly or hitting behind the runner, a stolen base, or a smart slide—whatever helps my team score runs .... The key is to be able to hit .280 or .290, drive in 120 runs, and still hit 30 to 35 home runs a year." Mike is proud he is a complete baseball player.

Sometimes, however, it is hard for fans to understand Mike. He is always so calm on the field. He is not a hot dog, a player who is a fancy show-off. He is calm. "I want to show everyone I have complete control of myself," Mike says. "To succeed as a hitter you have to have poise. If you are tense, you put pressure on yourself."

When fielding, Mike says if you are tense you'll commit more errors. You have to be relaxed and loose.

Mike looks cool and relaxed when he plays. But inside he is excited. He says he has to make sure he does not think about bad things that

Mike says that if he is tense, he will commit errors.

could happen. He tries to think about good things that will happen.

What advice does Mike give youngsters? He tells them to figure out what they want to do. He tells them to try everything. There are a lot of ways to be successful in life. Being successful does not mean you have to be a major league baseball player or pro football or basketball player.

"If you are happy, if you enjoy your life and have your health, those are the things that measure success in my book," Mike said. "I guess the Lord's purpose in my life was to be a professional baseball player, to be a good example."

And what does Mike tell young baseball players? He said they should just be themselves. He says be natural, stand at home plate the way it feels good, keep your eye on the ball, and try to hit it. He said not to try and be like anybody else. Don't say you're going to hit like Mike Schmidt or Pete Rose. Just have fun and learn teamwork and sportsmanship. When you get older there will be time to learn tips.

Mike is also a nice guy. He has curly red hair and he is handsome. Sometimes he is on television doing commercials.

Mike will sign autographs for fans, but he doesn't like to talk about himself. He is quiet and shy.

Mike plays basketball in his driveway. He has a big, beautiful house. He has a swimming pool. He has a Corvette and a Mercedes-Benz. He collects model railroad trains. To play for the Philadelphia Phillies in 1983 he is being paid $1.7 million.

He is a family man, too. He is close to his children. He has a son, Jonathan, and a daughter, Jessica. Mike has a purpose in life—to be as good as he possibly can at playing the game of baseball. He says he gets his strength from God.

Religion is a big thing to Mike Schmidt. "I have a solid Christian foundation," he said. "It's a commitment I have within my heart.

"I'm very lucky. Not many players are fortunate enough to have a life like I've had. Other players have had a lot more setbacks. I hope my career will be a good model for young kids. I hope I've been a player they would like to be like."

CHRONOLOGY

1949—Mike Schmidt is born on September 27 in Dayton, Ohio, the only son of Jack and Sally Schmidt.

1963—Mike graduates from the eighth grade of Loos School in Dayton.

1967—Mike graduates from Fairview High School, where he played football, basketball, and baseball.
Mike enters Ohio University in Athens, Ohio, without a scholarship.

1970—Mike, a junior at Ohio University, is named All-America in baseball.

1971—Mike finally gets a scholarship in baseball.
Mike graduates from Ohio University with a B.A. in business administration.
Mike is drafted in the second round by the Philadelphia Phillies.
Mike is sent to Reading, Pennsylvania, to play on the Phillies' AA team.

1972—Mike is sent to play on the Phillies' AAA team in Eugene, Oregon.
Mike is brought up to the Phillies at the end of the major league season to try out for the team. He plays in 13 big league games.

1973—Mike hits .196 in his rookie year.

1974—Mike marries Donna Wightman.
Mike is voted to play in the All-Star Game.

1976—Mike is again voted to play in the All-Star Game.

1977—Mike is voted a third time to play in the All-Star Game.

1979—Mike is voted a fourth time to play in the All-Star Game.

1980—Mike is voted a fifth time to play in the All-Star Game, but he does not play.
Mike is named the National League's Most Valuable Player and the National League's Player of the Year.
Mike is voted the Most Valuable Player of the World Series. The Phillies won the Series and Mike batted .381.
Mike leads the National League in runs batted in, 121.
Mike leads the National League in home runs, 48.
Mike is voted the Most Valuable Player of the World Series. The Phillies won the Series and Mike batted .381.

1981—Mike is voted a sixth time to play in the All-Star Game.
Mike leads the National League in runs batted in, 91.
Mike leads the National League in home runs, 31.
Mike is named the National League's Most Valuable Player for the second year in a row.

1982—Mike is voted to play in his seventh All-Star Game.
Mike wins his seventh Gold Glove award, the most ever by any National League third baseman.

1983—Only three players from the National League are selected to play in the All-Star Game and Mike is one of them. Mike leads the National League in home runs again.

ABOUT THE AUTHOR

Mike Herbert is a sports magazine editor. He has written and edited sports for 15 years. The magazines he edits are written for sports fans. They are: *Inside Sports, Baseball Digest, Basketball Digest, Bowling Digest, Football Digest, Hockey Digest, Soccer Digest,* and *Auto Racing Digest.* Mike Schmidt is one of the athletes Mr. Herbert admires very much.

Before he was a magazine editor, Mr. Herbert was an English teacher and a coach. He also played sports in high school and college. He has always loved sports. He still plays basketball and golf.

Mr. Herbert is married and has two children. His daughter Nancy, 16, plays on a high school badminton team. His daughter Susie, 9, plays soccer. His wife, Lana, is Susie's soccer coach. The whole family likes sports.

Mr. Herbert and his family live in Naperville, Illinois.